Lessons Beyond the Aisles not just a journey filled with stops and starts, ups and downs – it's about life. You might think this story is only for those interested in retail, an industry that's exciting, demanding, and often stressful. But you couldn't be more wrong.

If you're just starting out and unsure of your direction, this guide could be exactly what you need. It's not a textbook – it's a real-world roadmap. Step by step, it shows how a few simple behaviours can transform your life into a journey that's not just interesting, but genuinely exciting.

You don't need a degree. What you need is commitment to the job you're doing today, a desire to learn, and an eye for opportunity. This guide reveals all that – and more.

So if you're at the beginning of your career, take a moment to read this book. It might just change how you think, how you move forward, and how you chase your dreams. There's a lot waiting for you in these pages.

Give it a go – and start imagining what's possible.

Peter Noble

Former Head of Store Operations of Metro, China
Regional Fresh Manager of Metro, Vietnam
Operations Business/Country Manager of Panda,
Saudi Arabia
Territory Manager of Spinneys, Lebanon

Reading this book by Awais Awan took me right back to our days at Spinneys, Lebanon – those early years when we were building something real. I was just starting out, and Awais wasn't just my boss; he was a true leader.

We weren't simply selling groceries. We were shaping modern retail in a country coming out of civil war. Spinneys was the first organised chain in Lebanon, and under leaders like Awais, it became a training ground for many of us who went on to lead across the region.

This book captures all of that. It's a powerful journey through resilience, failure, grit, and growth. Awais was one of the toughest, most driven people I've worked with – and that spirit shaped everyone who shared that path with him.

This is more than a book. It's a story we lived. And I'm proud to have been part of it.

Ali El Zein
Country Manager, City Hypermarket, Qatar

Awais Awan's book speaks to every stage of the retail journey. From the grind of entry-level work to the strategic thinking required at the top. It's not just theory, it's real, practical advice based on learnings that actually work on the shop floor to the boardroom. If you are serious about building a career in retail, this book is your roadmap. If you ever doubted that retail can provide a fulfilling, exciting, lifelong career, read this book!

Tom Byrne
Managing Director, L Connaughton & Son's

This book is much more than a story rooted in retail – it's a powerful exploration of leadership, growth, and the human journey behind every role. Watching Awais progress from stacking shelves to becoming a respected global leader has always inspired me, but what truly moved me were the reflections at the end of each chapter. They brought out the emotional and personal realities of leadership – what it means to show up every day with resilience, dedication, and purpose for your team, your company, and your family. An invaluable guide for anyone building a meaningful career.

Imran Sheikh
Operations Manager, Amazon

Lessons Beyond the Aisles was a fantastic read that truly showcased Avi's timeline walking through the retail industry. The book was interesting, and informative. I learned so much more about Avi and the steps he went through to become the seasoned professional he is today. I especially enjoyed the "Reflection" section at the end of each chapter.

This is more than a book about Avi's life. This is a tutorial of patience, persistence, and perseverance of navigating through the retail environment. So many great learnings for someone just starting in the industry and a fun book to read even for experienced and tenured retail works. It brought me back to all the steps I've navigated and some of them very similar to those Avi wrote about.

Well done, Avi! I am proud to have been part of your journey.

David Rees
Circle K Worldwide Marketing

Lessons Beyond the Aisles

Avi Awan

First published in Great Britain in 2025
by Awais Awan Publications
avi2006@icloud.com

© Copyright Avi Awan 2025

ISBN (paperback): 978-1-9191734-5-0
ISBN (eBook): 978-1-9191734-2-9

To my wife and two boys, thank you for your love, patience and constant presence.

And to all those I've worked alongside throughout my career, I thank you for the lessons, the moments and the growth. Each of you has left a mark.

Contents

Author's Note

WHEN MOST PEOPLE THINK of retail, they picture tills, uniforms, and shelves being stacked. And yes, I've done all of that. But after more than 30 years in the industry, across seven countries and a wide range of roles, I've come to see retail differently.

It's not just a sector. It's a proving ground. It's where I've led multi-million-dollar businesses, sat in back offices solving problems before sunrise, and taken long-haul flights to unfamiliar countries in search of progress. It's also where I've made mistakes, had difficult conversations, and learned how to lead people, navigate cultures, and understand myself more deeply.

I've worked in roles with modest salaries and others with far more responsibility. But over time, I've realised the real currency in retail isn't money or title. It's people, pressure, pride, and the kind of growth you only notice when you pause to look back.

This book isn't a business manual. It's a personal reflection. A collection of stories and lessons that shaped me. Not from textbooks or boardrooms, but from shop floors, staff rooms, long drives between stores, and the quieter moments that often go unnoticed.

If you've ever led through uncertainty, grown through challenge, or questioned your own path, I hope this book gives you something to take with you. And if you're just beginning a journey in retail, I hope it shows what this industry can really mean.

Introduction

Why Write This Book?

I DIDN'T SET OUT TO WRITE a book.

In fact, I spent most of my career doing, not documenting.

From stacking shelves in the UK to leading retail operations across the Middle East, I was always focused on the next challenge, the next store opening, the next team to build.

But somewhere along the way – maybe in the quiet moments between flights or during late-night store checks – I realised how many stories I was carrying.

Not just about retail.

But about people. Culture. Mistakes. Transformation.

And growth.

This isn't a textbook.

It's not a playbook either.

It's a series of reflections – real moments from the shop floor to the boardroom.

Some are about strategy. Others are about failure.

But most are about learning.

Because retail is more than aisles and margins. It's about people.

And leadership is more than titles and targets.

It's about humility, presence, and the willingness to evolve.

If you're navigating change, this book is for you.

You may be in the middle of your journey, wondering if you're doing it right or if you even belong.

If that's you, maybe something in here will resonate.

Let's begin.

Chapter 1

The Start

SIX MONTHS' PROBATION. *I don't know if I'll make it.*

That was my first thought when I joined Morrisons as a part-time staff member.

I lacked confidence. I didn't know what good looked like. I didn't even know if I had what it took to survive in retail, let alone grow.

But I kept showing up. I worked hard, stayed curious, and paid attention.

The six-month deadline came and went. Slowly, I started getting recognition. It was electric.

The power of being seen

Recognition became a drug.

When I was growing up, love was constantly there but not always expressed in words. So, when someone at work said, 'Good job' or 'You've got potential,' it meant something. It drove me. I got into a rhythm – a flow – and I didn't want it to stop.

Then one day, I was asked if I wanted to supervise the casual staff.

No new title. No extra pay. Just a quiet acknowledgement I was ready to lead.

I jumped at it.

That moment – the joy of being trusted – I'll never forget.

After a few months, I applied for the official management training programme, but I wasn't accepted.

That hit hard.

Some of the people who got in didn't want it as much as I did. That was difficult to swallow, but maybe it wasn't luck. Maybe it was the right person seeing potential at the right time.

Syd Senior, my store manager, created his own training plan. I joined it and began learning by doing – rotating through departments, teaching myself, staying curious.

A different kind of flight

While all this was happening, I held onto a quiet dream I'd carried since being in the Air Cadets – to become a pilot.

It was never something I pursued, but the dream stayed with me, as a symbol of what I wanted life to feel like. To rise above, to stay steady, and to help others take off.

I never learned to fly a plane, but I was learning how to fly in my own way.

How to lead. How to navigate pressure.

How to help others take off.

I continued to rise at Morrisons. I was promoted, moved across different stores, and eventually helped open a new store. This involved training staff and building the operation from the ground up.

It was one of the proudest – and most pressured – moments of my early career.

That store opening caused immense strain. Many of the team had never worked in retail. I was still developing myself, but now I was expected to lead others. I enjoyed the challenge, but the intensity started to get to me.

That's when some former colleagues told me about a new retailer, Netto.

They said the company promoted autonomy, ownership, and growth.

I listened.

And when the opportunity came … I took it.

🛒 Reflections...

1. **A small spark can start it all.**

   You don't always start with a vision.

   Sometimes you start with a shift, a spark – the feeling of being seen.

   And that's enough to get moving.

2. **Recognition isn't fluff.**

   It's fuel.

   For someone unsure of their place, a few words can ignite belief.

3. **Leadership starts in the mirror.**

   Back then, I thought leaders had to be loud, feared, in control.

   What I didn't know was that true leadership starts in the mirror ...

   ... and sometimes, with a sincere apology to your younger self.

4. **Growth isn't always loud.**

   Promotions, new stores, big titles – they all feel like growth.

But real growth often happens quietly.

Late-night shifts. Coaching a new recruit. Choosing patience over pride.

5. **Leaving isn't always running away.**

Sometimes we leave because we're lost.

Other times, we leave because we're ready to – even if we don't know what's next.

Chapter 2

The Grind Behind the Growth

RETAIL HAD ALREADY started shaping me, but Netto took things to another level.

It was lean, intense, and relentless.

Running on empty

As deputy manager, I did it all – unloading deliveries, stocking shelves, serving at the checkout, locking up. Some days, I forgot to eat. One night, while placing a stock order for the store through the central distribution system, I nearly collapsed. I was so exhausted, I didn't realise my body had reached its limit.

That moment forced me to stop.

Morrisons had taught me structure, standards, and process. But Netto was something else. It taught me how to run a store with minimal support and maximum responsibility.

There were no layers, no teams of specialists. Just me and a small group holding it all together.

I was working six or seven days a week, often long shifts without breaks. I was learning everything, but I was also burning out. Still, the opportunity to be promoted to store manager wasn't something I took lightly. I accepted it with pride, pushing through the exhaustion.

And that's when I had one of the most humbling moments of my career.

My district manager at Netto rarely smiled. He was tough, old-school, and direct, with a presence that always felt heavy.

His wife used to shop at our store, and because of who she was, she carried herself with unspoken authority. The staff showed her a natural respect, but she often voiced unsolicited views, which at times disrupted the store's energy. Her presence felt commanding and not always constructive, but her influence was destined to fade.

When the roles reverse

One morning, I was opening the store, still half-tired, preparing for another long day.

To my surprise, the district manager arrived early. But this time, he was different. Softer. Quieter.

I made him a coffee. We stood there, awkwardly – two people used to fast conversations and direct feedback.

He cleared his throat. 'I've been given a choice: redundancy or a store manager role. I'm taking the role.'

And just like that, the hierarchy shifted.

Titles fade. But how you treat people doesn't.

Eventually, I realised I couldn't continue working the way I was. The intensity that helped me grow also taught me my limits.

It was time to move on.

 **Reflections...**

---

1. **You can't lead on empty.**

   Drive and discipline matter. But so does fuel. If you're burning out, it's not sustainable, no matter how strong your intentions.

2. **Growth without support has a cost.**

   Autonomy made me sharper. But it also made me tired. Every leader needs someone watching their back, not just their results.

3. **Pride fades. Character doesn't.**

   One day, the person who has led you may need your help. When that happens, show up with humility, not ego. That's real growth.

4. **The strongest leaders are often the quietest.**

   You don't need to be loud to lead. You need to be present. Focused. Consistent. And human.

Chapter 3

Out of Sync

AFTER THE GRIND of Netto, I joined Woolworths ... and stepped into another world.

A different kind of retail

Gone were the six-day weeks, the back-breaking deliveries, the speed, and the hunger. I walked into a world of non-food: toys, music, clothing, stationery, sweets. The pace was slow. The environment was calm.

Too calm.

And everyone seemed to have been there forever.

It was a well-oiled machine, and I was the outsider. They knew their jobs. I didn't know how to add value. It wasn't just uncomfortable. It was disorienting.

I struggled to adapt. I had gone from running full-scale operations to being placed on a structured training programme. It was the first time I'd been told to step back – not to lead, but to observe. That wasn't easy for someone used to learning by doing.

Even the numbers confused me.

People celebrated small percentage gains in key performance indicators (KPIs), but I couldn't understand the excitement.

The volume and scale didn't feel impactful. It all felt … distant. Detached.

Finding energy in the Golden Quarter

Still, I gave it time. I stayed open. And then came the Golden Quarter – Christmas.

The calm store turned electric. Customers filled every aisle, music blared, stock flew off shelves. I came alive again. There was action, movement, challenge. And the team responded with energy. Younger, more dynamic staff joined the holiday crew, and I connected better with them.

We rolled up our sleeves and got to work.

In that quarter, we won Best Store Standards in the district, and the buzz was incredible.

It reminded me: buzz comes in waves.

Even in the quietest environments, momentum can return if you hold steady long enough.

Just as I began feeling settled again, Safeway came calling.

They offered me a role in their management training programme.

It was a tough decision.

Part of me wanted to stay at Woolworths now I finally felt I was making an impact. But another part of me knew food retail was in my blood. And Safeway represented structure, systems, opportunity – and a return to the world I knew best.

I took the offer.

Even though I was moving forward, I took something with me: the knowledge that fit isn't always instant, but every chapter teaches you something.

 **Reflections...**

---

1. **When the fit isn't perfect, stay curious.**

   Misalignment doesn't mean failure. It means you're learning where you thrive – and where you don't.

2. **Sometimes stepping back is the real training.**

   Being told to observe instead of lead was frustrating. But it helped me see the business with fresh eyes.

3. **The buzz always returns.**

   Retail moves in rhythms. If the pace slows, it will pick up again. Hold your nerve. Stay sharp.

4. **Not all crossroads are obvious.**

I didn't know if I was making the right choice. But I followed what made me feel alive. And that's never the wrong direction.

Chapter 4

Back to Basics

SAFEWAY WAS A return to the world I knew – supermarket retail – but it had a structure I'd never experienced before.

From day one, I was placed on an intensive 16-week management training programme, with assessments every few weeks. It was up to me to absorb, apply, and deliver. I quickly realised I was good at learning fast, but that didn't always mean I was learning deeply. I passed the tests, but I didn't always fully own the knowledge.

Speed vs. depth

That was my first real insight: speed doesn't replace depth.

Safeway's structure wasn't built around traditional departments, but processes. That changed everything for me. Over time, I rotated through several key roles, each adding a different layer to my understanding of the business:

- **Replenishment manager:** I learned how to lead teams in setting the right standards, planning delivery routines, and ensuring availability was never compromised.

- **Systems manager:** I dug into automated ordering, inventory control, and the subtle details of how store systems make or break efficiency.

- **HR manager:** I handled recruitment, interviews, performance management, and all the people-side complexities I used to overlook.

- **Customer service manager:** I ran the fresh counters, managed customer flow, resolved complaints, and prepared for assessments that would define the store's performance.

Each process gave me insight and, more importantly, range.

As well as running a store, I was learning how to plan, execute, and analyse every aspect.

This was also when I saw the real power of internal stakeholders.

If one part of the process failed – the system, the order, the rota, the standards – something somewhere else would feel the effect. It was no longer only about doing your bit well. It was about connecting the dots across the business.

Passing the final stretch

I started working on projects, rolling out policies, leading action plans with SMART objectives, and thinking not just about what we were doing, but why and how we could do it better.

Safeway laid the foundation for me to become a business-minded store leader.

That all came to a head in the final stretch of the programme.

I had rotated through every process – replenishment, systems, HR, customer service – and had seen every side of the store. But the real test came in the form of a four-hour assessment by the area operations controller. It was rigorous. Nothing was off the table – numbers, systems, people, standards, and strategy were all covered.

And I passed.

What's more, I owned that moment.

It was the first time in my career I felt truly equipped. Not just to run a department but to lead a store.

Full circle

While I was preparing for that final step, life threw me a familiar face.

My former boss from Netto – the one whose wife used to walk our store like royalty – joined Safeway.

He needed help, and I supported him through his training.

No pride. No awkwardness. Just quiet support.

That moment grounded me. It showed me something I hadn't realised before.

Pride fades. Capability grows.

And, one day, you might be the person helping the one who once led you.

That's not a loss of power. That's the power of growth.

Reflections...

1. **You don't become a great store manager by doing one thing well.**

   You become a great manager by learning how everything connects – people, systems, service, and process – and making them work together.

2. **Quiet confidence comes from experience.**

   Passing that four-hour assessment wasn't about luck. It arose from weeks of pressure, process, and perspective.

3. **What you give comes back, even if the roles change.**

   Supporting someone who once led you shows grace. And grace is a powerful form of leadership.

4. **Retail teaches life.**

   Because at its best, retail isn't just about transactions – it's about transformation.

Chapter 5

Lebanon – The Leap

I ALWAYS HAD the desire to work overseas. On the surface this was a career move, but inside it was something deeper. I'd visited Dubai a few times as my father was doing business there, and something about the energy, scale, and ambition of the Middle East planted a seed.

That seed sprouted within me.

I began applying for roles abroad, focusing mostly on Saudi Arabia and the United Arab Emirates. I came across a vacancy in Saudi, and the recruitment consultant was fantastic. An interview was scheduled for Monday, and I was all set – train ticket booked, suit pressed.

Then, on the Friday, I got the call: 'It's cancelled – no visas available.'

As I trudged to the station to get my ticket refunded, the disappointment hit hard.

But I didn't give up.

Shortly after, I was contacted about a new opportunity – this time in Lebanon. I didn't know what to expect, but I said yes to the first-stage interview in London. The role was operations manager in a supporting role overseeing the store's systems and processes.

I arrived the night before and unpacked my things, only to realise … I had forgotten my smart trousers.

The interview in jeans

It sounds like a minor detail, but at the time – this was 1999, when wearing a full suit to an interview was the standard – it hit my confidence hard. I had to attend the interview in jeans.

I felt like I'd already failed before even walking into the room.

But then I saw the recruitment consultant was wearing jeans too, and I took it as a sign: maybe things will be okay.

The first stage went well. I was invited to the second round. That's when things got serious.

It would be a two-day assessment where, each day, seven candidates would be tested. In the afternoon, only three would be chosen for interviews – the rest thanked and sent home. We could choose which of the two days we wanted to attend.

I chose day two.

I explained the process to the cab driver that morning, on the way to the assessment centre.

He said, 'You'll do well.'

And strangely, I believed him. That gave me a lift.

When I arrived, I quickly realised the other six candidates were far more experienced than I was. Their backgrounds were impressive, their confidence obvious. I felt completely out of my depth.

So, I made a decision: I would just enjoy the day. Learn something. Treat it as experience.

One of the assessments was a five-minute presentation on customer loyalty. Luckily, I had worked on loyalty-related projects during my time at Safeway. We were given 20 minutes to prepare. I decided to structure mine using four simple questions: what, where, why, how. It worked.

There was a maths test next – incredibly tough. The kind of test that makes you feel like you're applying to NASA. But everyone struggled, so I didn't feel alone.

By lunch, I was relaxed. I'd made peace with the idea that I wasn't going to be chosen.

Then we were all asked to go downstairs and wait while they selected the top three.

I put on my jacket. Shook everyone's hand. Wished them well.

And then they called my name.

I'd been selected.

I sat waiting for the final interview, stunned. For the first time, I felt seen for who I was, not just for what was on paper. It wasn't about being perfect. It was about being honest. That moment stayed with me.

Before the interview, I took a personality test. The result surprised me – I was rated equal parts introvert and extrovert. They asked me why. I said, 'At work, I give it my all. But when I go home, I like my own space to reflect.'

In the interview, they asked me what I had learned from my career so far.

Owning your story

I told them a story about a poor inventory result at one of my early stores. Auditors had come in, and I realised how serious the situation was. I didn't hide anything from the interviewers. I shared the mistakes and what I learned from them.

They appreciated the honesty.

That interview didn't just open the door to Lebanon.

It taught me that sometimes, when you stop trying to impress, you finally connect.

Reflections...

---

1. **Sometimes a missed opportunity leads to the right one.**

   If the Saudi role had worked out, I may never have discovered what Lebanon had to offer.

2. **You don't need to be the most experienced person in the room, just the most grounded.**

   Everyone else had the CVs, but I had clarity. That's what carried me.

3. **Preparation matters, but presence wins.**

   In the end, it wasn't the trousers or the test that made the difference. It was showing up authentically.

4. **Humility isn't weakness.**

   When I stopped trying to win, I started to grow. And the door opened.

Chapter 6

The Lebanon Experience

THREE WEEKS AFTER the interview, the phone rang. I was offered the role.

There was no email back then. I waited for the official offer letter in the post, but truth be told, it didn't matter what it said. I had already made up my mind. I was going.

It was a huge moment for me and my family. We'd always lived in Yorkshire. My entire world – my parents, siblings, close friends, and everything familiar – was there. It was all I knew. I would be leaving that world behind and venturing alone to a strange country.

But I didn't hesitate.

At the airport, I was smiling. Joking. Almost too calm.

I don't think I had fully processed what I was doing.

I landed in Beirut in the evening. It felt unfamiliar, but not in a bad way. The airport, the drive to the hotel, the warm night air – I liked it. I checked in, unpacked, and went to sleep. This might just work.

But when I woke up the next morning, everything shifted.

I opened the curtains and looked out at a city I didn't understand, in a country people back home had warned me about.

Jokes had been made before I left:

'Will you need a helmet?'

'You sure it's safe?'

What was I doing there?

Why did I leave my family, my friends, the only life I'd ever known?

The farewell hugs, the pride in my parents' eyes – it all came flooding back.

And in that moment, I didn't feel brave.

I felt lost.

That first day was tough.

When I started work as operations manager, the team was welcoming and kind. But I couldn't see it. I was still in shock, mourning what I'd left behind. I felt low. Homesick.

It wasn't just culture shock, it was emotional dislocation.

But then something happened.

Within a week, I was handed an inventory project, then another. I got busy. I had responsibility. People needed me.

And somewhere in the middle of the work, without realising, I started to adapt.

I was still in a new world, but it was no longer foreign.

It was becoming mine.

Bombs and belief

One night during my first month, parts of Beirut's infrastructure – bridges and power stations – were bombed.

The sound was deafening, the shock immediate. I genuinely thought I was going to die.

I barely slept, assuming something worse would follow. When I turned up at work the next day, I was expecting chaos. But I walked into something else entirely.

People were calm and focused.

Meetings were already happening.

Discussions were underway – not about escape, but about staples: pulses, candles, rice.

Contingency plans were being made.

And I just sat there, stunned, processing my fear while everyone else had already moved forward.

That day changed something in me.

I realised resilience isn't just about surviving, it's about functioning in uncertainty.

Training the trainers

As I grew into the role, I was handed a huge opportunity: to build a management training programme from scratch.

It felt big. But I knew what to do.

I went back to what I'd learned at Safeway and mirrored the structure, adapting the content for the Lebanese market. Over time, we trained over 80 management trainees, many of whom would go on to hold regional and international leadership roles.

It became one of the most meaningful parts of my journey.

The SOPs I was scared to write

As the business expanded, I was asked to write process documentation and standard operating procedures (SOPs).

At first, I hesitated. I didn't feel equipped. But again, I returned to what I knew – the structure of Woolworths, the training tools of Safeway – and slowly, I started writing.

Eventually, I created SOPs, trained training managers, and introduced store audits to raise execution standards across the estate.

We weren't just managing anymore, we were measuring what we treasured.

The ERP experiment

Then came the biggest leap – an enterprise resource planning (ERP) implementation.

Requests for proposal (RFPs), shortlisting vendors, interviewing, awarding the contract, and rolling out the system – I was involved in every part.

I made plenty of mistakes.

But the learning was immense. It stretched my understanding of how systems integrate, how teams adopt change, and how patience is often the greatest project tool of all.

A culture that changed me

Looking back, there's one thing that shaped me more than any system or structure – culture.

I started out thinking leadership is universal. That tone, feedback, standards, and pressure work the same everywhere.

They don't.

In Lebanon, I had to learn how to read people, speak to values, and adapt without losing the heart of who I was.

For the first year, I got more wrong than right.

But my boss never let me go.

He could have. Maybe he should have.

But he saw something in me. And that belief became my bridge.

It was in Lebanon that I first truly understood:

Leadership isn't about power. It's about presence.

Especially when the culture isn't your own.

 **Reflections...**

---

1. **Courage often arrives after the decision.**

    At the airport, I was smiling. But the real bravery came when I woke up in Beirut and chose to stay.

2. **New beginnings often come with silent grief.**

    What no one tells you about change is how much you mourn what you leave behind, even if you're excited about what's ahead.

3. **Purpose pulls you through.**

    It wasn't comfort that helped me adjust; it was being given something meaningful to do.

4. **Adaptation isn't loud.**

    It doesn't arrive in a speech or a ceremony. It shows up quietly, in the middle of the work.

5. **You don't learn resilience by reading about it.**

    You learn it by surviving the shock – and still showing up to the meeting the next day.

6. **Systems build scale, but people build belief.**

   The SOPs, the ERP, the audits – they mattered. But what changed things was seeing people rise through the system.

7. **Culture isn't a barrier, it's a teacher.**

   You don't lead well until you understand how people interpret tone, status, trust, and truth.

8. **Staying is sometimes the bravest choice.**

   It's not always about taking the job. It's about staying when everything in you wants to go.

9. **Leadership isn't about always getting it right.**

   Sometimes it's about having someone believe in you long enough for you to figure it out.

10. **Adaptation happens while you're doing.**

    Change doesn't always feel like a choice. Sometimes it happens while you're busy trying to deliver.

Chapter 7

The Saudi Shift

I HADN'T BEEN looking – but Saudi Arabia was.

In 2004, the country was entering a new retail era. Hypermarkets were being built as anchor tenants inside malls. For many families, a trip to the mall was entertainment, and the hypermarket was the main attraction.

I was headhunted for a role at Panda, one of the largest retail chains in the region.

They were looking for someone who could lead from the floor up, understand the complexity of retail operations, and help shape a new way of shopping in Saudi Arabia.

I was ready.

From Dubai dream to Saudi reality

Years earlier, I had visited Dubai and stepped into a hypermarket that blew my mind.

It was massive – 11,000 square metres of scale and service. I remember thinking, *Whoever runs this must be something else.*

Now here I was, general manager of Panda's first hypermarket of that same size in Saudi Arabia.

It felt surreal.

A full-circle moment.

Immense gratitude flowed through me.

Running it all

This wasn't just a store. It was a business, and I was leading every function.

Marketing, commercial ops, HR, IT, finance, supply chain. All of it rolled up to one desk. Mine.

It was the first time I was truly accountable for the entire A–Z of a large-scale retail operation.

And I loved it.

But I wasn't doing it alone.

I had a team. A sharp, hungry group of leaders whom I coached, empowered, and challenged. We set KPIs together, created space for ideas, and built a culture where people took ownership of results.

And we delivered. Big time.

Lessons in culture, lessons in scale

Panda was full of talent from all over the world – South African, French, British, Saudi – with each person bringing a different layer of expertise. I absorbed everything.

- From the French, I learned about long-term planning. While we were opening stores in the UK with all hands on deck, they were already working on the next promotion – three months ahead.

- From the South Africans, I gained deep insight into supply chain and logistics. Precision, flow, and structure.

- From the British team, I learned the power of pragmatism – getting things done with clarity, urgency, and accountability.

- From the Saudis, I saw the importance of adaptability. They knew how to read the room, manage relationships, and move things forward even when the rules weren't written down.

Before I became general manager, mystery-shopper scores were consistently poor – hovering around 30%. After I took over, the scores didn't improve right away, and I started to question why.

Then I asked a simple question: 'Have we trained the team on what the mystery shopper is looking for?'

The answer was no.

I arranged training for all 400 staff, complete with role plays and practical walkthroughs.

When the next mystery shopper came in, we hit 80%.

From 30% to 80%.

I'll never forget the cheers in the team room that day. People stood taller. They realised they could move the needle.

That moment rippled across the company.

Not because I had the answers, but because we had finally asked the right questions.

Building leaders, not followers

We ran weekly team meetings where each department head shared their results.

But we took it further – rotating leadership so every team member practised presenting, leading, and owning outcomes.

I was developing future general managers, and I knew it.

The buzz in the team was something special. The culture was electric.

Many of those department heads are now vice presidents, directors, and C-level leaders across the region and even in the US. That's something I'll always be proud of.

Success – but still searching

As the results came in and my profile grew, I started to feel something strange.

I was doing well. I was respected. I had made a name for myself.

But something was missing.

I didn't have a professional qualification, and that started to bother me.

I decided to invest in myself and enrolled in an MBA in Retail Studies at the University of Stirling. It was a hybrid programme – mostly remote, but I travelled to Scotland several times a year for tutorials and exams, usually over weekends.

At the same time, I was promoted to operations business manager – the critical bridge between operations and head office. My job was to help build the infrastructure for hypermarkets and supermarkets across the country.

The learning curve was steep.

But by now, I was used to learning on the climb.

 Reflections...

---

1. **Sometimes the dream is already quietly shaping itself before you even know it.**

   The Dubai hypermarket I once admired? Years later, I'd be leading one just like it.

2. **Leading from the centre means owning everything – and trusting others to do the same.**

   Success came not from doing it all myself but from building a team that could think, act, and lead.

3. **Growth is about asking the right questions.**

   The mystery shopper score didn't improve until we stopped assuming and started training.

4. **Cultures don't clash – they complement.**

   The French way of planning, the South African systems mindset – every culture had something to teach me.

5. **Developing people is the real legacy.**

   The greatest pride comes not from the results you hit but from helping to create future leaders.

6. **Even during successful periods, keep checking in with yourself.**

   Respect and results are great, but don't ignore the quiet internal voice that wants to grow further.

7. **Investing in yourself is a decision, not a reward.**

   The MBA wasn't something I needed to get ahead. It was something I needed to feel whole.

Chapter 8

Return and Reframe

COMING BACK TO THE UK felt like returning to my roots. After eight years abroad, I had grown – professionally and personally. I now had a wife and a young son, and wanted to be closer to the wider family to give my son the kind of grounding I had known growing up.

It wasn't just a holiday. I had come back with the intention of finding a role. While visiting, I applied for a position with Makro UK and was invited to complete a SWOT analysis – 200 miles away.

I travelled there, analysed the store, and met the district manager.

He asked what I would need to focus on if I got the job.

I answered, 'Study the UK regulations again. It's been a while, and things change.'

He smiled at that.

A few days later, before returning to Saudi, I was called to an assessment centre.

I arrived at 9 a.m. and spent the entire day in assessments. At 6 p.m., I was called in for the interview.

Two days later, back in Saudi, I received the call. I'd been offered the role of general manager for Makro's Wolverhampton store.

Learning home all over again

Back in the UK, I joined a structured training programme, visiting various Makro stores, learning the systems, and sharing what I'd experienced overseas.

There was a mutual curiosity.

They wanted to learn from my global retail experience, and I wanted to understand how the UK had evolved in my absence.

My new district manager was German, also with international exposure. We understood each other's journey and became mutual sounding boards.

I brought with me a different way of looking at data.

I created performance sheets, added department-level graphs, and made sure the teams could actually see how they were doing.

Visual, shared, actionable – it changed how they engaged with the numbers.

Serving the HORECA customer

One of the customer groups I loved working with was HORECA – hotels, restaurants, and catering businesses.

I didn't just serve them. I visited them.

I walked into their kitchens, saw their prep, talked to their chefs. I wanted to understand their business so I could shape mine.

That feedback loop helped. It gave me insight into what mattered to them: availability, time, price, and flexibility.

When I joined, our store was at the bottom of the availability ranking. Through focus and teamwork, we climbed to third place.

We weren't perfect. But we were consistent and committed.

The call you don't expect

I was building something. The team. The customer base. The rhythm.

Then I was called to head office and informed the Wolverhampton store was being considered for closure. Its proximity to another location was cannibalising business.

The decision was made; it wasn't in our favour.

But the announcement was still to come, and I wasn't allowed to say a word until the next day at 4 p.m.

That day – walking the store, seeing my team, smiling, saying nothing – was one of the hardest days of my career.

At 4 p.m., the news was shared.

What followed was remarkable.

The team pulled together. Sales actually increased. Morale, strangely, stayed strong.

On one visit, an HR representative asked, 'How are they this motivated, knowing they're being made redundant?'

I didn't have a clever answer. I just said, 'I showed them respect. I considered who they are, not just what they do.'

We ran one-to-one consultations. We supported CV writing. We had open conversations.

I saw first-hand how fragile work can feel.

And how powerful dignity can be in difficult times.

The long drive

I was fortunate to be offered another store, which came with a two-hour commute each way.

That gave me time to think. To reset.

And to start again.

A new team. A new customer base of different businesses – some buying to resell, others purchasing ingredients for their restaurants.

I loved it.

I remember one product – wine with a short shelf life.

I searched our database, found out which customers regularly bought it, and called them. I offered them a deal. They were happy. So were we.

Makro and Metro: thinking globally

What I valued about Makro was that we weren't just a UK business.

We were part of the Metro Group, with teams and talent from across the globe.

I attended leadership courses with peers from different countries, and it was humbling to share ideas, challenges, and solutions across cultures.

It reminded me that the more places you lead, the more perspectives you gain.

And leadership is nothing if not a global language.

 **Reflections...**

---

1. **Coming home doesn't mean going backwards.**

   I returned to the UK with international wisdom and found new ways to serve, build, and lead.

2. **Numbers speak louder when everyone can see them.**

   Performance becomes shared responsibility when the data is visible.

3. **HORECA customers taught me the power of understanding the why behind the buy.**

   It's not just products; it's process, time, and trust.

4. **How you exit is as important as how you enter.**

   The store closure taught me that leadership is measured in the hard moments – in silence, empathy, and grace.

5. **Even when a chapter ends, character continues.**

   We couldn't stop the closure, but we led through it with heart.

6. **Long commutes can build long thoughts.**

   Sometimes the road becomes your classroom. Reflection needs space.

7. **Retail may be local, but leadership is global.**

   You often learn more when you step outside your market and into someone else's model.

Chapter 9

Oman – Behind the Duty-Free

AFTER COMPLETING MY MBA, I stayed connected with several people on the course. One of them was Tom, whose background was rooted in duty-free. We'd shared ideas during the programme, and when the UK retail market started to slow down and Makro's model was becoming less relevant, Tom reached out with an opportunity.

'Why don't you join me in Oman?' he said.

He'd been appointed as general manager for Muscat Duty Free, and they were expanding.

I thought about it, then made the move.

A different kind of Gulf

Oman was another Arabian Gulf country but with a completely different culture from Saudi Arabia. The people were kind, gentle, and respectful. But they were also deeply sensitive. A positive conversation could lift someone for a week. A harsh word could derail a relationship for a month.

Leadership there required emotional awareness as well as decisiveness.

I had to tune in, not just speak out.

Tom's presence and mentorship

From the very beginning, Tom did something different.

He shared videos about the history of duty-free, the psychology of the passenger, and the evolution of gifting and luxury shopping.

It wasn't just about understanding product.

It was about understanding people in transit – passengers who were emotional, often rushing, and looking to make meaningful purchases in a short amount of time.

We'd often walk the floor together, having coffee and talking through the store. These weren't formal meetings but ongoing, thoughtful conversations. He'd ask me who I saw as a 'star', who had potential. Those chats often turned into career conversations for the people we noticed.

Tom understood people.

And he helped me deepen how I understood retail.

Stakeholders everywhere

Duty-free was a new world, and the stakeholder list was long:

- My leadership team
- The airport authority
- Airport police
- Oman customs
- Oman Air (our partner)
- Inflight sales services
- Brand vendors (perfume houses, watchmakers, cosmetics brands)

It wasn't just about managing product and people, it was about orchestrating a business in someone else's space, under tight security, with very high expectations.

I also led our seaport store, where customer visits were entirely time-bound. Cruise passengers would dock, visit Muscat, rush into the duty-free department, and head straight back.

There was no time for long chats.

Service there meant speed, precision, and availability.

Understanding the passenger mindset

The duty-free customer isn't just buying. They're usually:

- Buying for someone else

- Shopping with emotion

- Racing against the clock

Perfume, luxury watches, cosmetics – these weren't just products. They were gestures. Gifts. Rituals.

Team members needed more than sales training.

They needed empathy, listening skills, and confidence in their product knowledge.

Some purchases were planned.

Others were impulse buys. And the quality of the team member made the difference between a missed opportunity and a meaningful sale.

Building the business from within

One of the first things I did was take two years of sales data and analyse category performance:

- What was moving

- What was stuck

- Why it was happening

- How we could adjust the range

I didn't want to guess. I wanted to understand.

We also introduced a Career Passport for every team member. This tracked:

- Which categories they were qualified to sell

- What their next steps were

- Where they wanted to grow

The moment we launched it, people started asking, 'What's next for me?' That curiosity was gold.

It gave people visibility – and it gave the business a powerful development map.

Some were trained in perfume, others in watches.

Some had natural energy for car promotions or gold raffles.

Now we could see it clearly, support it intentionally, and celebrate it visibly.

Operations at a new level

Duty-free retail came with its own complexities:

- A 24-hour operation

- Flight schedules that changed weekly

- Customs processes

- Access clearance (replacing a single sick staff member could be a 72-hour task)

If we didn't plan carefully, the whole system felt the repercussions.

Inventory control had to be tight, especially for high-value items.

We introduced cyclical stock counts and tight reconciliation, and we mapped customer trends by flight region. South Asian flights meant heavy confectionery volumes. European flights meant perfumes and luxury items.

We also linked our in-store point-of-sale (POS) system with pre-order systems, so passengers could order online and pick up their purchases on arrival or departure.

It was fast, complex, and constantly moving.

But it was incredibly fulfilling.

Leading with care

One of my biggest leadership breakthroughs came from a performance issue.

There was a manager who had been with the company a long time but wasn't performing.

Rather than opening with confrontation, I started with his job description.

I sat down with him and asked, 'Can you walk me through what you do, point by point? Where you're strong and where you need help?'

It changed the dynamic.

He realised we weren't there to blame him; we were there to support him.

Where he asked for help, I promised I'd deliver.

And I did.

Over time, that consistency built trust.

And trust brought change.

A note on family

Many of our team members were expats, living away from their families.

The store was their community; their colleagues were their family.

So, leadership meant more than performance.

It meant creating a safe, respectful, trusting space, where people felt seen, developed, and understood.

The commercial close of leadership

Every month, our finance manager would create a report and ask:

- Why did we win?
- Why did we lose?
- What did we learn?

I knew I'd be asked.

So, I got closer to the business on a daily basis, not just at month-end.

And when we reviewed the month, I didn't give opinions.

I gave reasons and next steps.

Operations and strategy became one conversation.

⊞ Reflections...

1. **Respect isn't just about how you speak, it's about how you follow through.**

   Saying 'I'll support you' is easy. Delivering that support – again and again – builds real trust.

2. **Duty-free isn't transactional. It's emotional.**

   People buy duty-free gifts with meaning. They're in transit, and that emotion lives in every sale.

3. **Team members shine when you let them see a path.**

   The Career Passport gave people purpose. And it gave leaders perspective.

4. **High-pressure environments demand emotional intelligence.**

   What works in one country won't work in another. Kindness, understanding, and awareness lead better than authority.

5. **Sometimes the best conversations happen while walking the floor.**

   Tom didn't teach in meetings. He taught by being present.

6. Stakeholder management is silent leadership.

You're managing partners, policies, airport police, and processes, while making it look seamless.

7. Commercial success starts with curiosity.

I didn't wait to be asked why sales moved. I asked myself – every day.

Chapter 10

Back to Saudi – Leading with Purpose

IN JANUARY 2012 I was approached for a new opportunity in Saudi Arabia – this time with a company called AFS. They operated over 60 stores across Western expat compounds and, more significantly, held a major contract with Saudi Aramco, serving large residential communities across five locations.

The stores were highly profitable, and Aramco was firm in its expectations. Under the terms of the contract, the stores had to be led by a Western expat with over 10 years of retail experience and an MBA. I happened to fit that exact profile.

AFS was persistent, and I later found out why. For every month the position remained unfilled, the company faced a financial penalty from Aramco. Their urgency eventually wore me down, and I took the role.

Thrown in fast

Barely two weeks into the job, I was assigned to visit every Aramco location to gather feedback from customers.

It felt like walking into a storm.

I was bombarded with complaints. People were frustrated, mostly about poor range, inconsistent fresh products, and a lack of international familiarity in the offering. These were expats from the US, UK, South America, South Africa, Australia, and more – all living in Aramco's highly secure compounds and expecting a retail experience that felt like a home away from home.

The pressure was immense.

Aramco wasn't just a client – it was a stakeholder with real contractual authority. If there was a complaint, they could fine us. And they did.

This meant I had to manage not just customers and staff but also Aramco's administrators, who were highly engaged and very particular about quality standards.

I was being judged by everyone, and it was overwhelming.

A mindset shift

I realised quickly that, to succeed, I had to mentally reposition Aramco as my boss.

That mindset alone helped shift everything – my communication, my accountability, my decision-making.

I made a conscious effort to remove headaches for them, not cause more. That meant listening, aligning, and acting fast. It also helped me build trust, which was essential in a partnership where perception and performance mattered equally.

Finding a way in – starting with fresh produce

With complaints flooding in and trust hanging by a thread, I needed to make an immediate impact. But where and how?

The breakthrough came when I realised that fruit and vegetables were a universal category. No matter what part of the world our customers were from, everyone needed fresh produce.

And, more importantly, we had access to it.

So, I decided to turn fruit and veg into our signature category.

We sourced better quality, expanded the range, and trained the team to continually check and maintain standards.

We focused on visual presentation, freshness, and seasonality, so customers saw something different the moment they walked in.

This wasn't just about product. It was about rebuilding perception.

If we could win their confidence in fresh produce, we could buy time to fix the rest.

And it worked.

Customers noticed the change.

It gave us breathing room – and belief.

A bold move

As I studied operations, I noticed something concerning.

Certain imported fresh products – especially from the UK – would sell out within two days. But due to the supply cycle, once out of stock, they wouldn't return for up to six months.

I knew we couldn't build trust with empty shelves, so I took a chance. I placed a massive order – so large that the leadership at AFS challenged me, and even the UK supplier called to double-check if I'd made a mistake.

To make it riskier, I followed it the next day with a second order, factoring in lead times and short shelf lives. It was a gamble. If the products didn't sell, the waste would cost me my job.

But my gut – and my understanding of the business – said otherwise.

And it worked.

Sales surged. Customers noticed the change. The entire perception of our fresh and imported ranges began to shift.

Building training into the culture

While operations improved, I knew our people needed development.

We had a trainer, but we lacked structure. So, I created a Toolbox Training programme: 10-minute modules delivered daily on specific topics. The goal was simple:

compound learning over time, with no excuses for missing out.

It became part of the store culture.

We also introduced certified training pathways so team members could earn qualifications and see a career path.

And the team responded. They began taking initiative.

The fruit and veg specialists redesigned displays by season.

The bakery team started producing unique items found only in our stores.

We were no longer just fixing operations; we were creating a retail identity.

Recognition and promotion

Eventually, I was called into a meeting with Aramco.

This time, it wasn't a complaint. It was to say thank you.

They recognised the improvements and acknowledged the effort. From a stakeholder known for their high standards and critical eye, this meant a lot.

I don't remember everything they said. But I remember how it felt – like I'd finally been heard.

No matter how high you are, recognition always helps. We're all human at the end of the day.

Shortly after, I was promoted to retail general manager, overseeing all AFS stores in the expat compounds.

New challenges, broader scope

This new role came with new complexity.

Each compound had its own dominant nationality – some Italian, others South American, others a blend. Every location was different.

Range once again became key.

You couldn't sell pasta without pasta sauce.

You couldn't offer top-ups without meal solutions.

So, I brought the same philosophy as I'd introduced in my first store:

- Start with fresh
- Build range based on local preferences
- Talk to customers
- Walk the stores

We turned small stores into community hubs, reflective of the people we served.

Expansion, data, and a costly oversight

I also led feasibility assessments for new compound stores. We'd review population size, income levels, rent models, and product demand to see if a new store made sense.

But not everything went smoothly.

We once opened a new site based on resident data that turned out to be wrong. Sales didn't come. We couldn't figure it out, until we noticed dusty parking bays and realised much of the compound was vacant.

That was a big lesson.

Never trust data until you verify it on the ground.

A strategic leap: UK market study

One day, the owner of AFS – a sheikh – called me in.

He was considering opening a store in the UK to serve the Arab community and wanted me to lead the market study.

I had never done this before.

I started by brainstorming with my team and realised I'd need:

- Realtors
- Accountants
- Freight-forwarding contacts
- Legal guidance
- Category analysis

I flew to London, walked the streets, booked three meetings with each type of partner to compare, and made detailed notes.

Each evening, the sheikh would meet with me.

He told me he was impressed, especially by my detailed groundwork. 'You didn't just arrive without a plan.'

I built a full feasibility plan and explored logistics, cost structure, and market appetite.

It didn't go ahead at the time due to other investments, but years later, I still believe that store would have been a huge success.

Working with PwC and building for the future

In my second year with AFS, I was asked to help redefine the retail strategy for the group.

We worked with PricewaterhouseCoopers (PwC), and it was a phenomenal learning experience. I learned the methodology of strategy building, how to structure stakeholder input, and how to present strategic roadmaps with clarity and cohesion.

We also revisited our ERP system, and I brought back insights from my Lebanon days, guiding the systems, and thinking with practical, experience-led direction.

Looking back

I still remember my first week at AFS – sitting across from frustrated customers, overwhelmed by expectations, unsure if I had made the right move.

But I kept going.

With every knock, I got up again.

And by the end, I had built teams, strengthened partnerships, taken bold risks, and stepped into a bigger version of myself.

This chapter wasn't just about turning a business around.

It was about discovering what kind of leader I was becoming.

Reflections...

1. **High expectations don't kill you – silence does.**

   Once you know what people really want, you can respond. Until then, you're just guessing.

2. **When the problem is everywhere, start with something universal.**

   Providing fruit and veg brought trust. That bought time. That changed the game.

3. **Treat your most demanding stakeholder as your greatest partner.**

   That mindset changes how you show up and how you're received.

4. **The biggest risks often come before the biggest wins.**

   I took a bet on inventory. It could have cost me everything. Instead, it earned me trust.

5. **Culture is built in 10 minutes a day.**

   Training doesn't need a classroom. It needs consistency.

6. **Recognition matters, even at the top.**

   Leadership can feel lonely. Being seen fuels you more than titles do.

7. **Data isn't always truth.**

   Verify in the real world. Always.

8. **Strategy is a language. Learn it.**

   Working with PwC gave me a toolkit I'd use for years to come.

Chapter 11

When Leadership Isn't Enough

THANKS TO THE progress we made at AFS, the company made a strategic pivot. Their investments shifted towards casual dining – a far more profitable area than retail – and I could understand why.

The retail side, particularly in the expat compounds, was becoming fragile. Store performance heavily relied on occupancy levels, which were dropping fast. Expats were leaving Saudi Arabia in large numbers, meaning lower footfall, dead stock, and locked-up working capital in stores that couldn't move their inventory.

The logical long-term option was to open stores outside the compounds. But that required a different kind of investment – larger, riskier, and longer term. In comparison, casual dining offered higher returns faster.

And so, the shift happened.

At the same time, I was approached by Meed Stores, a convenience chain with over 200 outlets. They were looking for a retail director – someone to take the business forward and create a scalable model. I was interviewed. They liked me. And I accepted.

Reality hits fast

I quickly realised I was stepping into something far more complex than a new title.

The retail director I was replacing hadn't delivered results and had been moved to the marketing department. But he wasn't exactly cheering for my success, because that would shine a light on his past failure.

From day one, I could feel the tension. His support, if you could call it that, came with undertones. And when you're brought in to fix what someone else left undone – and that person is still in the room – it rarely ends well.

But the bigger problem was what I had inherited.

There was no retail model in place.

I had over 200 stores but no unified system to check them against. No range blueprint. No merchandising standards. No supply chain consistency. No store format that could be scaled or copied. The question wasn't *How do I improve the model?* It was *What exactly am I improving?*

Deep structural cracks

Everywhere I turned, the same issues appeared:

- The two key categories in convenience – beverages and crisps – were dominated by a single supplier, who had locked down most of the shelf space, making it almost impossible to introduce new range or drive category development.

- Deliveries were direct from suppliers to stores, without proper checks. The risk of collusion was real – and happening.

- Stores had earned a reputation as tobacco shops, with cigarettes driving most of the traffic at razor-thin margins. That wasn't just bad branding, it was dangerous for the business model.

- And then there was the store design. Counters were placed at the entrance. Customers would walk in, buy cigarettes, and leave. No browsing. No flow. No chance to build basket size. I suggested relocating the counters at the back – to create movement, not friction – but the idea was shot down.

The operational foundations simply weren't there.

Culture and control

Despite these issues, the hardest part wasn't the stores. It was the culture.

My boss had no meaningful retail experience. He wielded power, often via demoralising WhatsApp messages early in the morning, targeting the wrong metrics, blaming the wrong people, and setting the wrong tone.

I was trying to build process. He was trying to manage perception.

I even suggested we build a 'model store' – a pilot we could test, refine, and replicate across the chain. A structured, process-led reset.

He agreed.

But all that happened was a shuffle. Stock was moved from one place to another. No standards were built. No systems were introduced.

It wasn't a model – it was a repaint.

The airport store wake-up call

I opened a new store at Riyadh Airport – a high-profile site with visibility and volume.

I was hands-on from start to finish. And what I saw during the process shocked me.

If I hadn't been there personally, it would have been a disaster. The capabilities simply weren't there. The people needed coaching. The execution needed structure. And the support teams weren't prepared.

That store became my wake-up call.

We weren't ready, in terms of capability, planning, or infrastructure. The range wasn't defined, the store layout lacked flow, stock arrived late, and the team wasn't equipped. Execution was disjointed. What should have been a smooth launch exposed how much work was still ahead and how urgently change was needed.

Starting to slip

I faded a little more with each passing week.

I wasn't aligned with the leadership.

The strategy changed by the day.

There was no clear path forward.

And soon, I wasn't just questioning the business, I was questioning myself.

How could I inspire a team when I was losing faith in the system?

How would I deliver results when the infrastructure didn't support their delivery?

And the answer came – not in an epiphany, but out of exhaustion.

The decision

I resigned.

They weren't expecting it and asked me to stay. But after just over a year in the role, I had already made peace with my decision.

And the relief was incredible. I had finally stopped swimming against a tide I couldn't change.

I left with no bitterness, just the understanding that not every battle is yours to fight, and not every company is ready to change.

Of course, that brought its own challenge: *What do I do next?*

And that's when I realised something I've carried with me ever since:

We don't escape challenge; we just exchange it.

Some challenges build us, others drain us.

And the wisdom comes in choosing which ones are worth pursuing.

🛒 **Reflections...**

---

1. **Titles don't protect you from broken systems.**

   Even as a director, if the foundations are weak – process, people, purpose – you'll spend all your energy surviving, not leading.

2. **Not everyone wants you to succeed.**

   Sometimes, your presence is a reminder of someone else's absence. Navigate with grace, but don't pretend the politics don't exist.

3. **Culture sets the temperature before you walk in.**

   No amount of energy, intelligence, or structure can thrive in a climate that's cold, inconsistent, or toxic. You either reshape it or suffocate in it.

4. **There's no glory in staying somewhere that dims your light.**

   Leaving isn't quitting. It's choosing to honour your energy and save it for where it truly matters.

5. **Every leader has a breaking point – not of weakness, but of wisdom.**

   Your breaking point is the moment you stop trying to fix what doesn't want to change and start protecting what you have left to give.

Chapter 12

Qatar – Small Market, Sharp Lessons

AFTER MY EXPERIENCE in Saudi, I returned to the UK with a fresh perspective and clarity about the kind of role I wanted next. I accepted an offer to join a pharmaceutical company in Saudi as operations manager. Everything was signed and set – until it wasn't.

The company was backed by a major investment group. And when it collapsed, so did the deal. Overnight, it all disappeared. That entire network of companies came tumbling down like a house of cards, and I was left back at square one, asking myself, *Now what?*

Three days to decide my future

Out of the blue, a recommendation came through from someone who had worked with a group in Qatar. They were looking for a country manager. I was invited to visit the business for three days and present my findings to the board.

It was nerve-racking. I was an outsider stepping into someone else's business, tasked with finding problems and suggesting solutions. But I did what I'd always done. I went to the floor, looked at the numbers, asked the right questions, and told the truth.

A few things stood out immediately:

- The profit-and-loss structure didn't reflect reality. Entire departments were budgeted, yet the products themselves weren't even stocked. There was a gap between planning and execution.

- The stores lacked a clear value proposition. What did they stand for? What did the customer experience say about who we were?

- The commercial head office team needed strengthening. In a small market like Qatar, range planning had to be tight, distinctive, and agile. Imported products were a major differentiator, but they weren't being leveraged properly.

I shared my findings with the board. There was some pushback. Fair enough – no one likes hearing what's broken.

But twenty minutes after the board stepped out to deliberate, they returned with an offer.

And I said yes.

The real work begins

At the time, the company had only two stores, with a third in the pipeline. I threw myself into the development of that third site – planning layouts, working with contractors, coordinating equipment suppliers, and making sure the store wasn't just built, but built with intent.

This was real hands-on retail.

No templates. No safety nets. Just grit and purpose.

We were part of the SPAR network, which had its own rhythm. SPAR International would visit regularly, offering support, tools, and frameworks for store development, category management, and marketing. These were some of the most valuable engagements I had – structured, smart, and full of perspective.

And yet, we were in a small market. Big players were already ahead – better real estate, stronger brands, more recognition. We needed to be sharper.

We were known for our Arabic bread, and one day, when the oven broke down, we had no time to lose. We sent our head baker to Lebanon to get the part directly from the supplier. That was the kind of agility we needed – bold, fast, and rooted in understanding what mattered to our customers.

We also worked on cultural engagement, inviting embassies to showcase their national product ranges. South African night. French cuisine corner. These events brought warmth and community, and made our stores feel personal.

But looking back, one opportunity still stands out.

We had the brand. We had the foundation. And as the master franchise for SPAR in Qatar – a business built on franchising – we had the perfect model at our fingertips.

But we didn't develop a structure others could adopt.

No plug-and-play framework. No scalable path to grow without shouldering all the cost complexity.

In hindsight, that should have been part of our strategy from the start.

When priorities shift

As time went on, we began to hear whispers – the company was looking to sell the business. At its core, this was a distributor-led company, and retail wasn't their primary game. If a sale went through, I knew I might not be part of the plan.

At the same time, my wife had an opportunity to take on a new role back in the UK. My kids were getting older. School decisions needed to be made. And the path ahead in Qatar suddenly looked ... uncertain.

Together, we made the choice to move back to the UK.

It wasn't easy, but it felt right. We chose alignment over ambition.

 **Reflections...**

---

1. **Strategy is only as strong as your operating reality.**

   Budgets don't mean anything if they're built on assumptions. The product must exist before the numbers.

2. **Brand without proposition is just decoration.**

If customers don't understand what makes your store special, then it isn't.

3. **Some of your best insights come from being new.**

Those three days before I joined the company taught me more than months of internal meetings could have.

4. **Leadership is knowing when to go all in – and when to walk away.**

I could have stayed and waited. But instinct and family guided me towards the next chapter.

5. **Not every missed opportunity is a regret.**

I still believe a franchise model could have transformed that business. But some lessons are meant to be carried forward, not corrected backwards.

Chapter 13

Quiet Rebuilding

WHEN I RETURNED to the UK, the world was entering one of its most uncertain chapters. COVID-19 changed everything – routines, roles, and expectations. It was as if the whole world was holding its breath.

For the first time in years, I wasn't leading a team, opening a store, or sitting in back-to-back meetings. I was home – with space to think, reflect, and ask myself deeper questions.

I decided to use the time intentionally.

I enrolled in a series of certifications: PRINCE2, Agile Project Management, and CAVA, a qualification that allowed me to assess vocational learners. At first, I wasn't sure where it would lead. I just knew I wanted to stretch myself – to see if there was a world beyond retail, or if I could bring new tools into the industry.

A healthy dose of curiosity was also at play.

I'd spent so many years learning through experience. Now I wanted to balance that with formal frameworks – to understand how structured project management worked, how agile methodology could be applied, and how learning outcomes were properly assessed.

At the same time, I found myself consulting.

One project involved a niche retailer investing in a new supermarket concept. I was brought in to advise on layout, merchandising, and process – all things I'd done many times before, but now I had the freedom to step back and guide from a higher vantage point.

Another assignment was with an independent retailer operating under a symbol group brand. He received corporate planograms and stock guidance, and I worked closely with him to help interpret and implement the information in a way that made commercial sense. It was an eye-opener for both of us – for him, in understanding the 'why' behind the layouts, and for me, in seeing how smaller retailers wrestle with big-brand systems while staying relevant to their local customer base.

There were no grand headlines during this period. No store openings. No new titles. But there was something else:

Quiet progress.

Reflections...

1. **Sometimes the biggest growth happens in silence.**

   Not every chapter is about momentum. Some are about stillness, reflection, and recalibration.

2. **You don't always need a job title to lead.**

   During my consulting work, I realised I was still leading, just without the badge. It reminded me that leadership is about impact, not position.

3. **Rebuilding isn't about rushing back; it's about coming back wiser.**

   That season gave me clarity. And when the next opportunity came, I wasn't just ready – I was stronger.

Chapter 14

The Promise of Guyana – Cut Short but Not Wasted

SOMETIMES AN OPPORTUNITY comes from a place you've never imagined.

I was scrolling through LinkedIn one evening and a post caught my eye: Country Retail Manager – Guyana, South America. I'd never considered working in South America before, but something about the role – the challenge, the uniqueness, the unknown – spoke to me.

The company was Penha, a well-established duty-free retailer operating across the Caribbean, selling perfumes, cosmetics, liquor accessories, and more.

Now, it was expanding into South America, and I was invited to shape the next chapter.

The application process was rigorous. Six interviews, psychometric assessments, personality profiling, background checks – the works. Every stage revealed something new about the business and its culture, and by the time the offer came, I was already invested.

But the world wasn't normal.

It was mid-COVID. Travel restrictions, documentation requirements, uncertainty everywhere. I had to get a special letter just to travel. This wasn't a standard relocation; it was a leap of faith into a country I knew little about, with no guarantees.

My first stop was Curaçao, where Penha's head office was based. It was stunning – a beautiful island with vibrant colours, kind people, and clear waters. But because of COVID restrictions, everything was closed. The streets were quiet. It was an eerie start.

After an induction and meeting the team, who were welcoming and professional, I moved on to Guyana.

That's when the culture shock hit.

Guyana was a country with immense promise. Its GDP was forecast to become one of the highest in the world due to recent oil discoveries. There was energy in the air – a sense that the country was on the brink of something massive.

But the infrastructure wasn't ready.

Importing products was a huge challenge. Delays, paperwork, and unpredictable customs rules all made the logistics of retail incredibly difficult. Yet, despite these hurdles, I felt something powerful in the people through their warmth, humour, and resilience. I loved their accent, though I sometimes struggled to understand them, and I found joy in their outlook on life.

I was assigned to open two new stores – one in a mall, the other at a local airport. I was on the edge of something exciting – a new frontier for modern retail in a fast-growing economy.

Life steps in

Suddenly, the view shifted.

A family member back in the UK became seriously ill. The work, the progress, and the challenge no longer mattered. I had to go home.

I flew back, not knowing how things would unfold. A few weeks later, the Guyana project was closed. The operation, given the import issues, infrastructure limitations, and now the lack of in-country leadership, was deemed unfeasible.

It was over before it had a chance to truly begin.

Back in the UK

Coming home should have felt like relief. But it didn't.

I carried anxiety with me – not just about what was next professionally, but the weight of everything happening around me. A family member's illness had triggered my return, and I was navigating unfamiliar emotions, uncertainty, and the quiet absence of routine.

And then there was something else – something personal.

When I had left for Guyana, my youngest son was two years old. He was like my key chain – always by my side. Walking through the airport without him had felt unnatural. I carried his absence in my heart the whole time I was away.

At the same time, I found myself deeply missing the Penha team. It had been a short stint, but something about the people – their warmth, openness, and professionalism – left a mark. It's rare to feel such an instant connection in a new role, let alone in a new country, but I did. They were, without question, one of the best teams I'd worked with.

While I was with Penha, I also had the opportunity to visit Miami to explore the logistics side of the business. It opened my eyes to another layer of retail – supply chains built around beauty, fragrance, and luxury. The warehouses were full of world-class products: perfumes, cosmetics, wines, spirits – and behind them, new people, new energy, and a fresh rhythm to how things were done.

Even though the Guyana chapter ended sooner than planned, I came away with a deeper appreciation for what retail looks like across cultures, across continents – and across emotions.

And even without a grand finish, that chapter left a quiet imprint I still carry.

 **Reflections...**

---

1. **Sometimes we make sacrifices quietly – not for applause, but because we believe we're building something better for the ones we love.**

    Leaving my youngest at two years old was one of the hardest things I've ever done. I often found my mind reaching for him, even when my hands were full.

2. **Some teams aren't just good at their jobs, they're good for your soul.**

   The Penha team was one of the most genuine and committed I've ever worked with. Their kindness, humility, and professionalism has stayed with me.

3. **Not every chapter ends with closure, but it can still end with gratitude.**

   I didn't finish what I started in Guyana. But I learned. I connected. And I came home with a heart full of pride and peace.

4. **We often think growth happens when we stay.**

   But sometimes, it happens in the going – and in the coming back.

Chapter 15

Navigating the Complex

WHILE I WAS still in the UK, I was consulting for a Saudi company when an opportunity came from Danube – a well-known chain of premium supermarkets and hypermarkets in Saudi Arabia, part of the BinDawood Holding group. They were looking for an operations director for the Riyadh region – the highest-performing and most commercially critical area in their network.

Unlike Guyana, traveling back and forth to Saudi was more feasible. After careful consideration, I took the role.

I arrived in Jeddah and found myself in the head office on day one, listening in on the weekly leadership conference call. The person leading it was Colin – the director I was set to replace in Riyadh. His grip on detail, presence, and confidence was clear. The guy was good.

Imposter syndrome niggled at me. I was stepping into his shoes, and they looked big.

Stepping in, finding ground

Before the official handover, I had an honest conversation with Colin, during which I asked, 'What are the key challenges I should look out for?'

He gave me a calm, professional overview. It was useful but made one thing clear: I'd need to figure the rest out for myself.

The handover concluded, and I began meeting the team – 21 store managers plus the wider support structure. My early strategy was simple: recognise wins, celebrate effort, and establish trust. I needed the team to see me as a coach, not a critic.

But it was a complex operation.

In many stores, large portions of space were sold to suppliers, who handled their own merchandising. That might sound efficient, but it came at a cost. Categories were fragmented. Like-for-like product comparisons were nearly impossible for customers. And as suppliers competed for visibility, store logic and flow often suffered.

To make things harder, merchandising disciplines weren't owned by store staff – they were outsourced to vendors, making it hard to enforce consistency. Rather than managing stores, I was managing a collection of competing visual agendas.

And then there was the internal dynamic.

The politics no one talks about

Most of the head office roles – particularly in the commercial team – were held by family members of the owners. You had to watch what you said and to whom you said it. One wrong sentence, in the wrong meeting, with the wrong person present ... and you'd find yourself in trouble.

It was politics without a playbook, and the stakes were always shifting.

One day, during a peak trading period, 10 to 15 people from head office arrived in Riyadh – unannounced – to audit every store. This team also managed central stock pushing, so they came in with preloaded narratives.

Their feedback was tough – direct and public.

Word got back to the COO in Jeddah. And to his credit, he flew to Riyadh the next morning to stand by me and the team. His name was Tony. We're still in touch. Good leadership leaves a mark.

The following Sunday, on the weekly call, the commercial team aired their criticisms again – this time to the full group. As Riyadh's lead, I spoke up and questioned if that was the right platform to raise operational issues. I challenged respectfully.

But that didn't land well.

Some of my Saudi store managers pulled me aside afterward and said, 'You shouldn't have challenged them. You should have agreed and moved on.'

That was difficult to hear. I had defended them, and yet it was seen as a misstep.

Still, I pressed on.

The whispers behind the walls

Things didn't calm down. In fact, they got stranger.

I'd occasionally receive direct calls from senior family members about issues in stores I hadn't yet heard about. Someone, somewhere, was reporting every small incident back to leadership. It was like there were unofficial 'watchers' in the stores, whose word carried more weight than the people managing them.

The message was clear: you're being observed, always.

I repeatedly asked myself how I was going to survive.

Not because I couldn't do the job – I was more than capable – but this wasn't a mood or a phase. It was the underlying culture.

Eventually, I made a decision. If this was the game, I'd learn the rules. I'd play smart. I'd adapt.

And I did. I became calmer, more considered, more strategic in what I said and how I said it.

That's when things began to shift.

One month later, after Ramadan and the Eid holidays, I received a surprise notification on my phone as I walked into the office.

I'd been given a bonus.

At first, I assumed it was an error. After everything – the store visits, the tension, the public call-out – it didn't make sense. But it wasn't a mistake. It was intentional. And it was generous.

I accepted it – gratefully and with quiet confusion.

The exit and the crossroads

Even with progress, something inside me had shifted. I had learned how to navigate the culture, how to thrive within it – but I no longer wanted to.

The role paid well. But I didn't want to sell my soul for a salary. Belonging isn't about adapting to every environment. Sometimes it's about realising: *This one isn't for me.*

Around the same time, a close friend of mine – someone I respected – had just been appointed CEO of Circle K. The irony? I'd been invited to interview for the same role two years earlier ... and turned it down.

Now he wanted me to join as country manager for Saudi Arabia and support Dubai's stores until the operation scaled.

He made a compelling pitch: 'Let's work as a tag team and disrupt the market.'

It felt fresh. Collaborative. Free from hierarchy games. After what I'd experienced, it was exactly the kind of air I needed to breathe.

At the same time, I received another offer – this one in the Caribbean. It was tempting. My heart was pulling towards it. But the financials didn't work.

In the end, I chose Circle K.

When I resigned, I expected a quick farewell. Instead, I received calls from across the organisation – from senior family members, store teams, and department heads.

They told me I was like family.

And I remember sitting with that thought for a long time. Because the way I'd often been treated didn't feel like family.

But maybe that's what maturity is – understanding that perception isn't always reality. Our experience sometimes bears no relation to how others see us.

Sometimes, you can be valued and still not belong.

I left with respect, some surprise, and a deep sense of what I no longer wanted to carry.

🛒 **Reflections...**

---

1. **Just because you've figured out a system, you don't have to stay in it.**

   Some roles teach you resilience. Others teach you release. Both lessons are valuable.

2. **Loyalty is a two-way street, but perception drives the traffic.**

   How we think we're viewed isn't always how others see us. That gap can shape everything.

3. **The right decision doesn't always feel rational.**

   My heart said Caribbean. My head said Circle K. In the end, the door I walked through led me to challenge and growth.

4. **Adaptation is a skill. Alignment is a choice.**

    I learned how to work within the system, how to speak the language, and how to navigate the politics. But knowing how to survive somewhere doesn't mean it's where you're meant to stay.

5. **Power without trust creates pressure, not performance.**

    When teams feel watched instead of supported, fear takes the place of creativity. And leadership becomes about survival, not progress.

6. **Sometimes leaving isn't walking away – it's walking towards yourself.**

    Choosing to move on from an environment that pays well but drains you isn't failure. It's clarity. It's knowing what you no longer want to compromise.

Chapter 16

Circle K – Fast Growth, Fractures, and Finding Myself Again

I RETURNED TO THE UK to sort out my visa for what was next – a fresh chapter with Circle K.

But before the new beginning came a sudden stop: I caught COVID.

I was bedridden for a week, exhausted, barely able to move. It was a low moment, physically and mentally, just as I was meant to be gearing up for a new role.

I landed back in Saudi, barely rested, and the grind started immediately.

During the first few days, I visited stores, sat with the CEO to review the business plan, and met the international franchise team at Circle K USA. They were great people who gave me a warm welcome. But I couldn't ignore the shift in mindset I had to make.

Just weeks before, I was running a hypermarket business with weekly turnovers in the millions. Circle K was different. Smaller store formats, different shopper missions, lower turnovers, and a business that was in early growth stages. It was humbling. One hypermarket could generate more in a day than all eight Circle K stores combined, but I quickly realised this wasn't a downgrade. It was a different game.

This was about scale.

About margin management.

About brand building from the ground up.

I had to unlearn some habits from big box retail and learn the art of precision retail – how to make a small space deliver big results.

A new world: coffee, doughnuts, and culture

One of the first things that struck me was the coffee culture. When I first walked into the store, I grabbed a Red Bull, and the barista asked if I wanted it mixed with syrup.

What?

But I tried it, and it was amazing (though dangerously high in calories).

Then I got curious.

I learned about V60 coffee – a method that takes 5–10 minutes to prepare, where grind time alters the flavour. I visited our bean supplier and got trained by the baristas. What started as curiosity turned into admiration. Coffee, I realised, wasn't just a drink. It was craft.

I began studying companion categories – doughnuts, croissants, cookies, cold drinks – and realised this is where the margins live.

So, we began developing our Food-to-Go range.

We partnered with a chef who truly understood the concept. He was talented and humble, and was building a full range for us. It felt like we had cracked the code.

But life interrupted again. He went on holiday to Egypt and tragically passed away from cancer. It was a shock. It reminded me how fragile things are – and how people, not just plans, shape a business.

We eventually restarted the project with our sister company and created a new range, but the original vision had changed. Still, the lesson stuck: it's not just about the product, it's about the passion behind it.

The race and the reckoning

Circle K's growth plan was ambitious. We had to expand fast – identify locations, conduct feasibility studies, get approvals, open stores, rinse and repeat. But the infrastructure wasn't scaling at the same pace. I flagged it. Others saw it too. But we kept pushing.

One particular week, we took over three fuel-station stores in just seven days. We weren't ready. Systems, teams, logistics – all were strained. And the stress hit the people first. Messages flying, mistakes made, gaps exposed.

I was also attending board meetings, but what we shared on paper wasn't always what was happening on the ground. I found that frustrating. I've seen what good looks like, and I knew this wasn't it – not yet. And that was on me. I should have been more vocal, more confident in challenging what I knew wasn't sustainable.

I was caught between pushing ahead and holding ground.

Friendship, friction, and finding the exit

The CEO was a close friend. We had been aligned before, but working together was harder than either of us expected. He was from an athletic background and had a driven, relentless, high-performance mindset. That works when the team is capable, but in a startup, that mindset can clash with capability gaps.

Some team members were great. Others came from completely different industries and were still learning. We were hiring fast and firing fast. The culture was forming on the go.

We opened over 20 stores across two countries, plus two franchise stores. We even won the Golden Spoon Award for Most Admired Convenience Retailer in Dubai. From the outside, it looked like a win.

But internally, the pace cost us.

It cost me.

An opportunity to go to the Caribbean came up again. I was tempted. But I stayed – again – because I wanted to finish what I'd started.

Then the CEO resigned due to health reasons.

I had worked with the incoming CEO before, though not closely. He came across great on LinkedIn, and I respected his background. But once we worked together, it was clear the chemistry was off. He brought in his own team. They began examining the operation, and naturally, the cracks started to show.

It was painful to have to justify everything and feel exposed over issues I had flagged months earlier.

Only one person acknowledged what I had carried. That meant a lot.

When my contract came up for renewal, I knew it was time to go.

It wasn't just about misalignment. I'd started receiving interest from companies outside the region – opportunities I couldn't explore while under contract. And, after everything, I needed breathing space.

Not to escape, but to reset. To reflect, recalibrate, and stay open to what might come next.

It wasn't something I shared back then, but it quietly shaped my decision.

And in hindsight, giving myself that space was one of the best decisions I made.

That space gave me something I hadn't felt in a long time: perspective.

And with it came the freedom to choose what was next instead of reacting to what was in front of me.

Leaving Circle K wasn't the end of something. It was the beginning of remembering who I was.

Reflections...

1. **When scale outpaces structure, you don't grow – you scatter.**

    We thought we were building momentum. But without a strong foundation, momentum just becomes speed. And speed without alignment creates chaos.

2. **Hire for attitude, yes. But in startups, hire for know-how too.**

    We believed in giving chances, and I still do. But when you're building from scratch, you need people who know how to build. Culture is key, but competence builds the scaffolding.

3. **Good leadership isn't loud. It's consistent.**

    I should have spoken up more. Challenged more. Trusted my experience instead of second-guessing it. Staying quiet to avoid tension only delayed the inevitable.

4. **You can love people and still not work well with them.**

    Friendship and leadership don't always mix. And that's okay. Sometimes, the relationship is healthier outside the business than inside it.

5. Never let a title silence your instincts.

I knew when things weren't working. I felt it. And I ignored it.

Next time – I won't.

Chapter 17

The Dutch Detour – Space to Think, Room to Breathe

AFTER LEAVING CIRCLE K, I returned to the UK and within a week, I was in the Netherlands.

I had been approached for a short-term project by a respected fuel company that was planning to take back control of convenience stores operating on their forecourts. These stores had been rented out, but now the company wanted to bring them under its own management. It was a fascinating project – one that let me return to what I do best: strategy, retail structure, and building something meaningful from the ground up.

What made this different, though, was the headspace.

This time, I wasn't buried in a thousand WhatsApp messages. I wasn't firefighting. I wasn't trying to hold up an entire business. I had the freedom to observe, think, and contribute – and that shift gave me a deeper appreciation for the power of focus.

Getting my eye back

In those first few weeks, I walked stores, spoke to stakeholders, studied the customer missions, and started to assess what was working and what wasn't. I made notes and created an early view of pricing, range, and category performance.

Then I met one of the Netherlands' most respected retailers – someone who had been watching the market for years. We sat down, and I shared my conclusions.

To my surprise and satisfaction, we were aligned.

He validated everything I had observed. That moment was huge. After a long stretch of self-doubt and internal battles, my confidence rose again. *I do see clearly. I do understand this space. I am still good at what I do.*

Strategy in iterations

I put together a strategy plan – not a 100-page document, but something clean, directional, and rooted in what I'd seen. We agreed to work in iterations. Test. Measure. Adjust.

We weren't chasing awards. We were building a framework.

It was liberating.

We reviewed store formats, range simplification, promotional strategy, and visual merchandising. I met key retailers who had already been acquired by the group, and again, our thinking matched. These were the kinds of conversations I had missed: practical, humble, and constructive.

Technology, walking, and the small things

In between store visits and planning sessions, I attended a retail technology show focused on AI, automation, and emerging trends. And because I wasn't weighed down by operations, I could absorb it.

I was inspired.

I walked over 40,000 steps that weekend, exploring and reflecting – just being present. It reminded me how much I'd neglected the simple things. The mental clarity that comes from movement. The ideas that arrive when the noise dies down.

We often glorify the grind. But clarity is born in thinking time.

Reflections...

---

1. **Confidence doesn't always come from praise. Sometimes it comes from alignment.**

   When others validate what you see – not to flatter you, but because they see it too – it reminds you of your value.

2. **Retail doesn't always need reinvention. Sometimes it just needs clarity.**

    I wasn't here to rip up the playbook. I was here to simplify it.

3. **There's a difference between being busy and being productive.**

    For the first time in a long time, I could think, not just react. That space gave me sharper insight than any 12-hour shift ever could.

4. **Small things aren't small. They're sacred.**

    Walks. Fresh air. A quiet cup of coffee. These aren't distractions. They're where you reconnect with the part of yourself that gets lost in the noise.

Chapter 18

Where I Stand,
and What I've Learned

I DIDN'T PLAN this chapter.

When I started writing, I thought I was just capturing stories – moments from the shop floor, lessons from the boardroom, fragments of a journey spanning countries and careers. But as I reach this point, I realise I've been doing more than that.

I've been making sense of it all.

The wins. The failures. The people who lifted me. The people who tested me. The moments I doubted myself, and the moments I found my voice again. Every country, every company, every chapter added something. And strangely, it's only now, looking back, that I see the thread that runs through it all.

It's not just about retail. It never was.

It's about growth.

About learning to lead when things are unclear.

About finding your rhythm in cultures you didn't grow up in.

And about remembering that, no matter how many titles you collect, it's the people who make the journey worthwhile.

But there's something else too.

Something I wish I had done more of, and sooner.

Reflection.

I always thought it was a fluffy word. Something you hear in a coaching seminar. Something people say but don't really do. But writing this book changed that for me.

Because for the first time in years, I wasn't just doing – I was feeling.

And feeling forced me to pause. To sit with those moments.

Not just the wins. But the regrets. The doubts. The risks I didn't take.

The parts of me I pushed to the side because I was too busy chasing the next store opening, the next profit-and-loss statement, the next project.

In writing this book, I met myself again.

Not the title. Not the job role.

Me.

And what surprised me most?

I didn't always like what I saw.

There were times I felt proud.

But there were also times I felt deep sadness. Sadness that I didn't give myself time earlier.

Time to learn. To walk. To be present with my kids.

Time to say no.

Time to just be human.

I used to think self-reflection was about looking in the mirror.

Now I know it's about seeing yourself without the filters.

And the only way to do that is to write from your soul, not your head.

Because your mind will try to judge it all.

But your soul? It will simply tell the truth.

What I've learned

1. **Leadership is not about having the answers. It's about asking better questions.**

    The more I tried to control everything, the less connected I became. Real leadership is about creating space for others to shine, to stumble, and to grow.

2. **Pace can be your enemy.**

    I thought fast meant successful. But fast often meant reactive, and reactive often meant shallow. The best decisions I made came from stillness, not speed.

3. **You don't have to burn out to prove you care.**

   For years, I wore stress like a badge of honour. But looking back, the moments that mattered most – to my teams and my family – came when I was calm, present, and real.

4. **Your story only makes sense in reverse.**

   At the time, some roles felt like detours. But now I see how every chapter gave me something I needed, even if it took years to understand this.

5. **Your gut knows. Always.**

   Time and time again, my instincts whispered a truth my mind tried to override. Whether it was about a role, a decision, or a person, my gut was never wrong. I just needed the courage to follow it.

What I'd do differently

If I could go back, I'd give myself permission sooner.

Permission to slow down.

To keep learning.

To invest in myself as much as I invested in the business.

To take those walks.

To capture my thoughts each week – not just for a book, but to stay in touch with myself.

A note to my younger self

You're going to feel like you don't belong.

That others are better spoken, better educated, better suited.

But your strength is your grit.

Your instinct.

Your ability to connect.

Your ability to learn through the doing.

Don't try to be polished. Just be present.

You'll get knocked down – many times.

But you'll get up every time.

And one day, you'll look back and realise:

You didn't just survive this journey.

You built it.

When your gut speaks, listen.

It knows you better than your mind does.

It's not reckless. It's honest.

Follow it, even when it feels scary.

Especially then.

What matters most now

I don't know what the next chapter holds.

Maybe it's a new market or a new way of working.

But I know this: Whatever I do next must align with who I am, not just what I can do.

Because I'm no longer chasing roles.

I'm chasing rhythm. Meaning. Wholeness.

And I want to live the rest of my story awake.

Not just achieving, but aware.

Chapter 19

Aisles and Beyond

I CALLED THIS book *Lessons Beyond the Aisles* for a reason.

Because for all the lessons I've learned about business – about operations, strategy, stakeholder management, culture, growth – the most important lessons weren't about retail.

They were about me.

About how you lead when no one's watching.

About how you show up when you're tired, or doubting, or stuck.

About how you treat people who have no power over you.

And about what happens when you stop long enough to reflect.

This book was never meant to be a blueprint.

It was never '10 steps to success' or 'how to lead like a boss'.

It was a journey. A real one.

With its mess.

Its mistakes.

Its quiet moments of pride.

And if there's one thing I've learned, it's this:

We're all in the aisles.

Some of us are navigating new countries.

Some of us are leading teams for the first time.

Some of us are questioning everything we thought we knew.

But we're all pushing our own trolleys, figuring it out as we go.

And the aisles – they teach you things.

They humble you.

They shape you.

They bring people into your life who challenge you, change you, and sometimes walk with you longer than you expected.

But beyond the aisles – beyond the KPIs, the store openings, the board meetings – there's something more.

Clarity.

Choice.

The person you're becoming.

So, if you've made it this far in the book, thank you.

Not just for reading, but for walking with me through this journey.

If anything I've shared helped you pause, or feel seen, or feel less alone in your own path, it was worth writing.

I'm still walking.

Still learning.

Still reflecting.

And finally giving myself the time to do it all with a little more presence, and a little more purpose.

Here's to what comes next.

For both of us.

Closing quote

'You don't always choose the path.

Sometimes the path chooses you.

But if you keep showing up, keep learning, and stay honest with yourself,

the journey will teach you everything you didn't know you were looking for.'

—Avi Awan

A note to myself

You've spent your whole life leading, solving, building – for others.

This book became something different.

It became a space to finally see yourself.

In these pages, you've written about markets and stores, KPIs and strategy.

But between the lines, you wrote something more important –

the parts of you that were tired, that kept going anyway,

that didn't ask for much,

but gave so much.

And now you see it.

So, to the version of me who kept moving even when it was hard:

I'm sorry I didn't stop to ask how you were doing.

I'm sorry I didn't listen to your gut sooner.

And I'm sorry I thought proving myself meant forgetting myself.

But now I know.

I know your heart's in the right place.

I know your instinct is your superpower.

And I know – more than anything – you deserved this moment.

To pause.

To feel.

To write.

To remember who you are.

This is not the end.

It's the beginning of something deeper.

With care,

Avi

Chapter 20

Reflections Beyond the Aisles

WRITING REFLECTIONS AT the end of each chapter wasn't part of my plan, but as the stories unfolded, the reflections started writing themselves.

Small truths. Big lessons. Quiet moments that left lasting marks.

This chapter brings them all together – not to summarise the book, but as a companion for your own journey.

Take what you need. Leave what doesn't land.

And maybe, like I did, you'll find clarity in the pause.

1. **A small spark can start it all.**

   You don't always start with a vision. Sometimes you start with a shift, a spark – the feeling of being seen. And that's enough to get moving.

2. **Recognition isn't fluff.**

   It's fuel. For someone unsure of their place, a few words can ignite belief.

3. **Leadership starts in the mirror.**

   Back then, I thought leaders had to be loud, feared, in control. What I didn't know was that true leadership starts in the mirror ... and sometimes, with a sincere apology to your younger self.

4. **Growth isn't always loud.**

   Promotions, new stores, big titles – they all feel like growth. But real growth often happens quietly. Late-night shifts. Coaching a new recruit. Choosing patience over pride.

5. **Leaving isn't always running away.**

   Sometimes we leave because we're lost. Other times, we leave because we're ready to – even if we don't know what's next.

6. **You can't lead on empty.**

   Drive and discipline matter. But so does fuel. If you're burning out, it's not sustainable, no matter how strong your intentions.

7. **Growth without support has a cost.**

   Autonomy made me sharper. But it also made me tired. Every leader needs someone watching their back, not just their results.

8. **Pride fades. Character doesn't.**

One day, the person who has led you may need your help. When that happens, show up with humility, not ego. That's real growth.

9. **The strongest leaders are often the quietest.**

You don't need to be loud to lead. You need to be present. Focused. Consistent. And human.

10. **When the fit isn't perfect, stay curious.**

Misalignment doesn't mean failure. It means you're learning where you thrive – and where you don't.

11. **Sometimes stepping back is the real training.**

Being told to observe instead of lead was frustrating. But it helped me see the business with fresh eyes.

12. **The buzz always returns.**

Retail moves in rhythms. If the pace slows, it will pick up again. Hold your nerve. Stay sharp.

13. **Not all crossroads are obvious.**

I didn't know if I was making the right choice. But I followed what made me feel alive. And that's never the wrong direction.

14. **You don't become a great store manager by doing one thing well.**

You become a great manager by learning how everything connects – people, systems, service, and process – and making them work together.

15. Quiet confidence comes from experience.

Passing that four-hour assessment wasn't about luck. It arose from weeks of pressure, process, and perspective.

16. What you give comes back, even if the roles change.

Supporting someone who once led you shows grace. And grace is a powerful form of leadership.

17. Retail teaches life.

Because at its best, retail isn't just about transactions – it's about transformation.

18. Sometimes a missed opportunity leads to the right one.

If the Saudi role had worked out, I may never have discovered what Lebanon had to offer.

19. You don't need to be the most experienced person in the room, just the most grounded.

Everyone else had the CVs, but I had clarity. That's what carried me.

20. Preparation matters, but presence wins.

In the end, it wasn't the trousers or the test that made the difference. It was showing up authentically.

21. Humility isn't weakness.

When I stopped trying to win, I started to grow. And the door opened.

22. Courage often arrives after the decision.

At the airport, I was smiling. But the real bravery came when I woke up in Beirut and chose to stay.

23. New beginnings often come with silent grief.

What no one tells you about change is how much you mourn what you leave behind, even if you're excited about what's ahead.

24. Purpose pulls you through.

It wasn't comfort that helped me adjust; it was being given something meaningful to do.

25. Adaptation isn't loud.

It doesn't arrive in a speech or a ceremony. It shows up quietly, in the middle of the work.

26. You don't learn resilience by reading about it.

You learn it by surviving the shock – and still showing up to the meeting the next day.

27. Systems build scale, but people build belief.

The SOPs, the ERP, the audits – they mattered. But what changed things was seeing people rise through the system.

28. Culture isn't a barrier, it's a teacher.

You don't lead well until you understand how people interpret tone, status, trust, and truth.

29. Staying is sometimes the bravest choice.

It's not always about taking the job. It's about staying when everything in you wants to go.

30. Leadership isn't about always getting it right.

Sometimes it's about having someone believe in you long enough for you to figure it out.

31. Adaptation happens while you're doing.

Change doesn't always feel like a choice. Sometimes it happens while you're busy trying to deliver.

32. Sometimes the dream is already quietly shaping itself before you even know it.

The Dubai hypermarket I once admired? Years later, I'd be leading one just like it.

33. Leading from the centre means owning everything – and trusting others to do the same.

Success came not from doing it all myself but from building a team that could think, act, and lead.

34. Growth is about asking the right questions.

The mystery shopper score didn't improve until we stopped assuming and started training.

35. Cultures don't clash – they complement.

The French way of planning, the South African systems mindset – every culture had something to teach me.

36. **Developing people is the real legacy.**

    The greatest pride comes not from the results you hit but from helping to create future leaders.

37. **Even during successful periods, keep checking in with yourself.**

    Respect and results are great, but don't ignore the quiet internal voice that wants to grow further.

38. **Investing in yourself is a decision, not a reward.**

    The MBA wasn't something I needed to get ahead. It was something I needed to feel whole.

39. **Coming home doesn't mean going backwards.**

    I returned to the UK with international wisdom and found new ways to serve, build, and lead.

40. **Numbers speak louder when everyone can see them.**

    Performance becomes shared responsibility when the data is visible.

41. **HORECA customers taught me the power of understanding the why behind the buy.**

    It's not just products, it's process, time, and trust.

42. **How you exit is as important as how you enter.**

    The store closure taught me that leadership is measured in the hard moments – in silence, empathy, and grace.

43. Even when a chapter ends, character continues.

We couldn't stop the closure, but we led through it with heart.

44. Long commutes can build long thoughts.

Sometimes the road becomes your classroom. Reflection needs space.

45. Retail may be local, but leadership is global.

You often learn more when you step outside your market and into someone else's model.

46. Respect isn't just about how you speak, it's about how you follow through.

Saying 'I'll support you' is easy. Delivering that support – again and again – builds real trust.

47. Duty-free isn't transactional. It's emotional.

People buy duty-free gifts with meaning. They're in transit, and that emotion lives in every sale.

48. Team members shine when you let them see a path.

The Career Passport gave people purpose. And it gave leaders perspective.

49. High-pressure environments demand emotional intelligence.

What works in one country won't work in another. Kindness, understanding, and awareness lead better than authority.

50. **Sometimes the best conversations happen while walking the floor.**

Tom didn't teach in meetings. He taught by being present.

51. **Stakeholder management is silent leadership.**

You're managing partners, policies, airport police, and processes, while making it look seamless.

52. **Commercial success starts with curiosity.**

I didn't wait to be asked why sales moved. I asked myself – every day.

53. **High expectations don't kill you – silence does.**

Once you know what people really want, you can respond. Until then, you're just guessing.

54. **When the problem is everywhere, start with something universal.**

Providing fruit and veg brought trust. That bought time. That changed the game.

55. **Treat your most demanding stakeholder as your greatest partner.**

That mindset changes how you show up and how you're received.

56. **The biggest risks often come before the biggest wins.**

I took a bet on inventory. It could have cost me everything. Instead, it earned me trust.

57. Culture is built in 10 minutes a day.

Training doesn't need a classroom. It needs consistency.

58. Recognition matters, even at the top.

Leadership can feel lonely. Being seen fuels you more than titles do.

59. Data isn't always truth.

Verify in the real world. Always.

60. Strategy is a language. Learn it.

Working with PwC gave me a toolkit I'd use for years to come.

61. Titles don't protect you from broken systems.

Even as a director, if the foundations are weak – process, people, purpose – you'll spend all your energy surviving, not leading.

62. Not everyone wants you to succeed.

Sometimes, your presence is a reminder of someone else's absence. Navigate with grace, but don't pretend the politics don't exist.

63. Culture sets the temperature before you walk in.

No amount of energy, intelligence, or structure can thrive in a climate that's cold, inconsistent, or toxic. You either reshape it or suffocate in it.

64. **There's no glory in staying somewhere that dims your light.**

Leaving isn't quitting. It's choosing to honour your energy and save it for where it truly matters.

65. **Every leader has a breaking point – not of weakness, but of wisdom.**

Your breaking point is the moment you stop trying to fix what doesn't want to change and start protecting what you have left to give.

66. **Strategy is only as strong as your operating reality.**

Budgets don't mean anything if they're built on assumptions. The product must exist before the numbers.

67. **Brand without proposition is just decoration.**

If customers don't understand what makes your store special, then it isn't.

68. **Some of your best insights come from being new.**

Those three days before I joined the company taught me more than months of internal meetings could have.

69. **Leadership is knowing when to go all in – and when to walk away.**

I could have stayed and waited. But instinct and family guided me towards the next chapter.

70. **Not every missed opportunity is a regret.**

I still believe a franchise model could have transformed that business. But some lessons are meant to be carried forward, not corrected backwards.

71. **Sometimes the biggest growth happens in silence.**

Not every chapter is about momentum. Some are about stillness, reflection, and recalibration.

72. **You don't always need a job title to lead.**

During my consulting work, I realised I was still leading, just without the badge. It reminded me that leadership is about impact, not position.

73. **Rebuilding isn't about rushing back; it's about coming back wiser.**

That season gave me clarity. And when the next opportunity came, I wasn't just ready – I was stronger.

74. **Sometimes we make sacrifices quietly – not for applause, but because we believe we're building something better for the ones we love.**

Leaving my youngest at two years old was one of the hardest things I've ever done. I often found my mind reaching for him, even when my hands were full.

75. **Some teams aren't just good at their jobs, they're good for your soul.**

The Penha team was one of the most genuine and committed I've ever worked with. Their kindness, humility, and professionalism has stayed with me.

76. **Not every chapter ends with closure, but it can still end with gratitude.**

I didn't finish what I started in Guyana. But I learned. I connected. And I came home with a heart full of pride and peace.

77. **We often think growth happens when we stay.**

But sometimes, it happens in the going – and in the coming back.

78. **Just because you've figured out a system, you don't have to stay in it.**

Some roles teach you resilience. Others teach you release. Both lessons are valuable.

79. **Loyalty is a two-way street, but perception drives the traffic.**

How we think we're viewed isn't always how others see us. That gap can shape everything.

80. **The right decision doesn't always feel rational.**

My heart said Caribbean. My head said Circle K. In the end, the door I walked through led me to challenge and growth.

81. Adaptation is a skill. Alignment is a choice.

I learned how to work within the system, how to speak the language, and how to navigate the politics. But knowing how to survive somewhere doesn't mean it's where you're meant to stay.

82. Power without trust creates pressure, not performance.

When teams feel watched instead of supported, fear takes the place of creativity. And leadership becomes about survival, not progress.

83. Sometimes leaving isn't walking away – it's walking towards yourself.

Choosing to move on from an environment that pays well but drains you isn't failure. It's clarity. It's knowing what you no longer want to compromise.

84. When scale outpaces structure, you don't grow – you scatter.

We thought we were building momentum. But without a strong foundation, momentum just becomes speed. And speed without alignment creates chaos.

85. Hire for attitude, yes. But in startups, hire for know-how too.

We believed in giving chances, and I still do. But when you're building from scratch, you need people who know how to build. Culture is key, but competence builds the scaffolding.

86. Good leadership isn't loud. It's consistent.

I should have spoken up more. Challenged more. Trusted my experience instead of second-guessing it. Staying quiet to avoid tension only delayed the inevitable.

87. You can love people and still not work well with them.

Friendship and leadership don't always mix. And that's okay. Sometimes, the relationship is healthier outside the business than inside it.

88. Never let a title silence your instincts.

I knew when things weren't working. I felt it. And I ignored it.

Next time – I won't.

89. Confidence doesn't always come from praise. Sometimes it comes from alignment.

When others validate what you see – not to flatter you, but because they see it too – it reminds you of your value.

90. Retail doesn't always need reinvention. Sometimes it just needs clarity.

I wasn't here to rip up the playbook. I was here to simplify it.

91. There's a difference between being busy and being productive.

For the first time in a long time, I could think, not just react. That space gave me sharper insight than any 12-hour shift ever could.

92. Small things aren't small. They're sacred.

Walks. Fresh air. A quiet cup of coffee. These aren't distractions. They're where you reconnect with the part of yourself that gets lost in the noise.

93. Leadership is not about having the answers. It's about asking better questions.

The more I tried to control everything, the less connected I became. Real leadership is about creating space for others to shine, to stumble, and to grow.

94. Pace can be your enemy.

I thought fast meant successful. But fast often meant reactive, and reactive often meant shallow. The best decisions I made came from stillness, not speed.

95. You don't have to burn out to prove you care.

For years, I wore stress like a badge of honour. But looking back, the moments that mattered most – to my teams and to my family – came when I was calm, present, and real.

96. Your story only makes sense in reverse.

At the time, some roles felt like detours. But now I see how every chapter gave me something I needed, even if it took years to understand this.

97. Your gut knows. Always.

Time and time again, my instincts whispered a truth my mind tried to override. Whether it was about a role, a decision, or a person, my gut was never wrong. I just needed the courage to follow it.

Acknowledgements

WRITING THIS BOOK has been one of the most humbling journeys of my life.

To every team member, leader, mentor, and even challenger I've crossed paths with – thank you. You helped shape the stories, the lessons, and the reflections that fill these pages. Whether it was a passing conversation or years of collaboration, each interaction left its mark.

To my family – your support, patience, and belief in me have been the quiet strength behind every chapter of my career. Thank you for understanding the late nights, the relocations, the moments I was there but not always present.

To those who saw something in me, even when I didn't – your faith gave me courage.

And finally, to the people who reminded me that I write well – your words stayed with me longer than you know. You triggered something I never expected: the decision to stop, reflect, and put it all down. This book wouldn't exist without that nudge.

A special thank you to Debbie Emmitt for her meticulous line and copyediting. Her attention to detail and commitment to clarity have significantly enhanced the readability of this book. You can find more about her work at www.debbie-emmitt.com.

A heartfelt thank you to Zara Thatcher for her brilliant work on both the proofreading and typesetting of this book. From start to finish, Zara has been incredibly supportive. She guided me through each stage of the process with patience, clarity, and care. Her attention to detail, responsiveness, and calm professionalism made the entire journey smooth and stress-free. An amazing professional to work with. You can find out more about her work at: www.printreadyeditorial.com

Thank you, all of you.

About the Author

AVI AWAN IS a global retail leader with over three decades of experience in the UK, the Middle East, and beyond. He has worked in seven countries, gaining hands-on experience across supermarket retail, convenience formats, duty-free, B2B, wholesale, and HORECA channels.

His journey began on the shop floor in Yorkshire and took him through hypermarkets in Saudi Arabia, airport retail in Oman, and startup ventures in South America. Along the way, he's opened stores, led turnarounds, built teams from the ground up, and learned how to lead across cultures and complexity.

Known for his grounded style and people-first mindset, Avi brings a blend of operational grit and quiet reflection to everything he does. His story isn't polished – it's lived.

Lessons Beyond the Aisles is his first book – a personal and professional memoir shaped by decades of doing the work and learning from it.

When he's not supporting retail businesses or mentoring future leaders, Avi enjoys long walks, writing, and rediscovering what really matters.

He wrote this book not to teach but to reflect – and to offer readers a companion for their own journeys through change, uncertainty, and growth.

www.ingramcontent.com/pod-product-compliance
Lightning Source LLC
Chambersburg PA
CBHW071651210326
41597CB00017B/2184